You can know that you have ....

Eternal
Life

By   Eugene W.Emmerich III

Eternal Life
by Eugene W. Emmerich III

Printed in the United States of America
ISBN-13: 978-1484826232
ISBN-10: 148482623X

Cover and interior design by Cheryl Fernandes, and Eugene Emmerich.
Cover art by Thomas Kinkade
Back photo by Todd and Brad Reed
Editing by Richard Carlson, and Special Bird 07.

Other books by the author available on Amazon:
CSI Jerusalem
Stargate 2
The Resurrection-Rapture

Life or Death Publisher

Table of Contents

A Brief Explanation

A Brief Explanation

If a friend of mine is about to drink something that they think is nutritional, but I know is poisonous, don't I have a responsibility to tell them? And if a friend has a terminal illness and I know of a cure, wouldn't telling them of the cure be my logical response? And if I had dined at a fabulous cuisine where the food and drink were amazing, wouldn't I tell others about this so that they could experience the taste for themselves? In the past I have written books with the intention of proving something to the reader. I presented my case as if a jury were going to deliberate on a verdict. As I endeavor to write on the subject of eternal life I want to do it not to prove something, but rather to tell a friend of what I understand to be true. I've spent most of my adult life researching this subject and feel that I have a good understanding of how the concepts of eternal life fit together. Even though I've never died or interviewed someone who has, I feel I understand death and how a person can pass from death to life. I have come to understand that the gift of eternal life, the passing from death to life can only be found in the hands of God. As I come to Him searching I learn of the joys associated with knowing Him and being known by Him, being loved by Him as a son.

So as you read the following pages I hope that you too will taste and see that the Lord is good. After you have read this book I hope you will experience for yourself what it feels like to be a child of God and to know that your Father gives you eternal life and will raise you from the dead some day. I hope you will experience the peace and contentment that comes from knowing you have an inheritance from God that is incorruptible, and can't be stolen. One that is irrevocable and unalterable. An inheritance that is reserved in heaven for you until the work of God is fully realized in you and complete.

In the following chapters I will warn of something that is lethal, advise of something that is the remedy, and point in a direction so that the reader can find out for themself if what I say is true and if there is someone named Jesus of Nazareth who is alive and can be known. I want to provide the reader with the opportunity to experience the love that I have experienced in a real relationship with the Lord. Just as it is hard to explain exactly how chocolate tastes to someone who has never tasted it, it is hard to explain exactly how the joy of knowing Jesus tastes. You have to taste for yourself to truly know.

If a person doesn't want to know the experience, God will honor their choice. The problem with that is; this is a life or death issue. We are gambling with our lives when we make these decisions. For the reasons briefly stated here I implore you to please consider what I have to say. Unless this is also your area of expertise please examine my observations with the consideration that they may be true and correct. If you started reading this book I'm asking you to please read it to the end and then decide what you think.

    Thank you

      Gino

Where Do We Start

Where Do We Start?

"All roads lead to God". Have you ever heard someone say this? I believe this statement is in fact true. All roads do lead to God but, all roads don't lead to eternal life. Yes, one day we will all stand before God and yet, not all of us will enter into his kingdom. So the question I will attempt to answer in this book is this: What must I do to receive eternal life? If I get all of life's questions answered correctly but get this one wrong then all of the other questions I answered correctly become irrelevant. Jesus made this point by asking the question, "What will it profit a man if he gains the whole world but loses his soul?"[1]

Yes, I believe this is the ultimate question in our lives that needs to be addressed. What is eternal life and how do I receive it? What happens when we die? As I examined what I believe to be true about eternal life I noticed that when Christians try to explain the process of gaining eternal life, or entrance into heaven, it's usually done in a language foreign to many non-Christian listeners. It is similar to the language of law that lawyers use to communicate with one another, or the language used to communicate between a doctor and a pharmacist.

---

[1] Mark 8:36

It's understood by most in house if you will, but to those outside of their community it's a method of communication that's hard to understand. In this book I will try to eliminate that type of language as much as possible.

As I share my observations about eternal life it will be done with the understanding that the source I'm using in most cases, the New Testament Gospels, are in fact historical documentation by people who claimed to be eyewitnesses of the resurrection of Jesus. These people claimed to have heard his words and saw the miracles that He did. Also, one of the writers (Luke) claims not to have been an eyewitness but rather an investigative reporter who's account collaborates with the accounts of the eyewitnesses. Another account is given to us by (Paul) a man who was putting the followers of Jesus to death but later became a follower himself. Paul's writings on eternal life come from the teachings of Jesus through the twelve Apostles and agree with the testimony of the eyewitnesses.

As I proceed I will occasionally examine terminology that is commonly used, but that may contain some misleading ideas that have been associated with these terms. I will examine questions that were asked of Jesus and the Apostles when they spoke on this subject, and I will examine some of the illustrations that Jesus used when trying to clarify what he meant by eternal life and how it is obtained.

I will attempt to connect the dots to show how eternal life is associated with resurrection from the dead, entrance into the kingdom of God, and a relationship with God on a personal level. I'm not doing this so as to redefine what is true but rather to provide another vantage point in an effort to gain a different perspective. An observatory that will make things easier to see or easier to understand than the ones used in the past riddled with in-house language and prejudices.

One of the writings of John, Jesus' closest companion and student, contains an interesting passage that speaks to the issue of eternal life. It goes like this:

And this is the testimony of God: that he has given us eternal life, and this life is in His Son. He who has the Son has life; he who does not have the Son of God does not have life. These things I have written to you who believe in the name of the Son of God, that you may know that you have eternal life

I John 5:11-13

As I write I will reflect back to the phrase in this passage, "He who has the Son". But the observation I'd like to make here concerns the motive for John writing this. He states, "I write these things.... so you may know that you have eternal life". It appears his stated objective is that the reader won't need to guess whether he has eternal life or not but that he can be sure of it. As I proceed with this exposition I want to do it with the same idea in mind; that you may know whether or not you have eternal life. If you are not sure about this today, then my hope is when you're done reading this book you will be.

Here is a question that I'd like to throw out there so it is in the back of our minds as we proceed. The question was asked by a rich young ruler of Jesus, "What good thing must I do to inherit eternal life?" The answer Jesus gave had more to do with the attitude of his heart than the good thing he thought he must do.[2] The question simply put is: What must I do? What is required? The question asked is about "eternal life", but in Jesus' answer, He refers to it as "entering into the kingdom of God". A few verses later He referred to eternal life as being "saved". Jesus makes being saved, entrance into God's kingdom, and having eternal life synonymous.

---

[2] Luke 18:18-27

What did He mean when He said saved? Saved like you save something on your hard drive, like saving money for a rainy day? No, I believe that the term saved relates to saved from death. Thus the second half of the equation would be, receive eternal life. The one who does this saving would be referred to as a savior (The Lord and Savior Jesus Christ).

The phrase, "pass from death to life" is used by both Jesus and John in the New Testament and is a phrase I can identify with. In the next chapter I will share more insight on the concept of passing from death to life, and I will do a short study on two spiritual laws; The law of sin and death and, the law of the Spirit of life.

Two Spiritual Laws

Two Spiritual Laws

For the law of the Spirit of life in Christ Jesus has made me free from the law of sin and death.

Romans 8:2

This is a passage from the book of Romans that tells us about two spiritual laws: The law of the Spirit of life in Christ Jesus, and the law of sin and death. The observational questions I need to answer here are, "what is the law of life and the law of death that the writer is referring to, and how are these two terms defined? Second, what is a spiritual law?" OK, the last question first. If we think of natural laws as facts that exist in nature, such as the law of gravity or, the laws of thermodynamics, or quantum physics, then we should think of spiritual laws in the same way, laws that exist in the spiritual realm. These laws would pertain to spiritual things. They apply to us as humans beings because we are not just a physical body but we are partially composed of soul and spirit. Soul and spirit being that human part you can't see but you know it exists.

I am assuming that from my brief explanation you understand what a spiritual law is. So with that in mind I'll continue examining the Romans passage I opened with. First I want to address the law of sin and death. This law creates a problem that the law of the spirit of life remedies. The law of sin and death can be simplified like this: If you sin you die. This was the message in the Adam and Eve story, "If you sin by partaking of the tree of the knowledge of Good and Evil you will surely die." What God said is evidenced in the fact that everyone who is born will eventually die. Look around and be sure. If you sin you die right? Since everyone from Adam and Eve has died or will die I think we can safely say without being judgmental, that everyone has sinned. OK, so the next logical question is; what does the word sin mean? Here is the definition of sin found in my Vine's Expository Dictionary of New Testament Words.

Sin (Noun and Verb)

1) Noun, Hamartia

is literally, "a missing of the mark," but this etymological meaning is largely lost sight of in the NT. It is the most comprehensive term for moral obliquity.

Obliquity meaning: A deviation from a straight line, plane, position, or direction. In a scriptural sense it's a deviation from direction as defined by God.

However, to keep the understanding of sin simple throughout our study I'll refer to sin with it's literal definition which is: a missing of the mark. One last point I need to make that I don't want to be lost in the simplification of our definition is this; "Missing the mark" doesn't mean that we are simply poor marksmen. Sometimes missing the mark is the result of not even aiming at it. We can miss the mark whether we are trying to hit it or not. I can miss the will of God in either case.

There are two passages in scripture I like that explain the problem caused by the law of sin and death and they too are found in the book of Romans.

Therefore, through one man Adam, sin entered the world, and death through sin, and thus death spread to all men, because all have sinned

Romans 5:12 The law of sin and death

For the wages of sin is death, but the free gift of God is eternal life through Jesus Christ our Lord.

Romans 6:23 The law of sin and death, and the law of the spirit of life

Later I will look at the contrast between wages and free gifts but right now I would like to summarize the law of sin and death. As I stated earlier the law works like this: if you sin you die. The Romans five passage says it this way, death is a consequence of sin and because all men sin (miss the mark), all men die. The chapter six passage refers to death as a wage, something that is earned in contrast to something that is given freely. But the chapter five passage nails it when it describes the results of sin like a disease that has spread to all men, a sort of spiritual and physical terminal illness. Not only is there a physical death but a spiritual death as well.

So now, what about "The Law of the Spirit of Life in Christ Jesus"? What does that mean? Well, the Romans six passage contrasts "death from sin" with, "eternal life from Jesus". Remember I brought up the phrase, "pass from death to life"? Well, Jesus is the remedy for death and not only does He have the words of eternal life but the remedy of life. He says he gives those who follow him eternal life and he will resurrect them from the dead.[3] If death comes from sin then life comes from Jesus. By Him we are able to pass from death to life.

---

[3] John 6:40, 6:68 and 10:27,28

Jesus said, "I give them eternal life", with the emphasis on "I GIVE THEM." We don't give it to ourselves, right? What person has ever given them self eternal life and avoided death... passed from death to life? Or which dead person can make them self alive again by doing some good deed and thus, pass from death to life? No one! It can't be done. It's a spiritual law that can't be changed or avoided.

In conclusion of this chapter, I hope it is understood what the law of sin and death, and the law of the spirit of life in Christ Jesus are. Many people might believe these things to be true but by merely understanding the facts we don't pass from death to life. We don't receive eternal life by acknowledging, "The facts are correct!" So what did Jesus mean when He said, "Believe on Me and you will receive eternal life"? Think about it for a while. I will address this important question in another chapter. In this chapter I have defined sin, and how it relates to the law of sin and death. In the next chapter I will look at how these two spiritual laws affect the dichotomy of man, and describe how the mechanics of these two laws are evidenced in us?

The Dichotomy of Man

The Dichotomy of Man

(Passing from death to life)

What is eternal life and how does it relate to the dichotomy of man? What I mean is; there is an outer man that can be seen, physical, tangible, of flesh and bones. But there is also an inner man that cannot be seen, invisible, yet real. The inner man is that part of you that exists even though you can't see it, but you know it's there. When you look in the mirror you don't see it but are aware of its presence. It is evidenced in what we call behavior and personality. The inner man is a combination of both soul and spirit. At this time however for the sake of simplicity, I want to stay focused on the dichotomy of man and eternal life as it relates to each of the inner and outer parts.

In the last chapter I discussed briefly the two spiritual laws; the law of sin and death and the law of the Spirit of life in Christ Jesus. Now I want to look at how these laws affect both the inner man and the outer man.

First; **The law of sin and death** and,
<u>The outer man</u>. We can easily see the evidence of the law of sin and death in the outer man in that all people eventually die and their bodies return to the earthly elements they were made from. Decay and decomposition. We see that physical death comes one per customer and cannot be avoided. It can't be transferred to someone or something else.

Second;
The inner man. The inner man is also infected with the disease of death. Many times the writers of the new testament refer to us as being dead in our sins.[4] The death described in the inner man isn't as easily evident but can be seen with a closer examination.

I think the easiest way to illustrate this is to examine the evidence from the heart of man. The man who doesn't want anything to do with Jesus or the things of God reveals a spiritual deadness in his heart. This condition can be observed at a personal level and collectively at a social level. The position in society that rejects God's moral standard and redefines life and morality is in opposition to the spirit of God. It reveals spiritual deadness that is in opposition to the Spirit of Jesus Christ. Spiritual death is evidenced by a non-desire to be one of His disciples. Jesus said, "If you're not with Me you are against Me."[5] So again, not wanting anything to do with Him is evidence of spiritual death in the inner man. Furthermore, some people see themselves as spiritually aware, but spiritual awareness and spiritual regeneration (passing from death to life) are not the same thing. I can be spiritually aware and still be infected with death, spiritually dead.

---

[4] Ephesians 2:1,5 Colossians 2:13
[5] Matthew 12:30

Now, the next question to be asked and answered is; how does the outer man pass from death to life and how does the inner man do the same? Do both happen at the same time? If not, when? In other words; how does the law of the spirit of life affect the inner and outer man?

First; **The law of the Spirit of life** and, The inner man. As I stated earlier the inner man is made up of soul and spirit. The two things are one, inner man. Even though the spirit of God sustains all life the inner man is dead. So how does the inner man pass from death to life? How does it work? Easy. Jesus is eternal. He is from everlasting to everlasting as described by the prophets of old. At a point in time when a person asks Him for eternal life He comes and indwells them, lives *in them*, in a way different from times past when God dwelt *with the people* in the temple. It is written, that at this point in time a person becomes the temple or tabernacle of God and is no longer exclusively their own. In the same chapter it is written, that this person now becomes "one spirit with the Lord". Just as two people become one in sexual union, the spirit of man and the Spirit of the Lord become one.[6] Since Jesus and his Spirit are eternal and I become one spirit with Him, his eternalness becomes imparted in me, a kind of engrafting process. My life in the inner man becomes eternal.

---

[6] I Corinthians 6:16-20

I have been spiritually regenerated, or as many have heard the phrase, "Born again". The inner man has passed at that point in time from death to life.

Second;
The outer man. The effect of the law of the Spirit of life in Jesus won't be realized, or evidenced as a reality in the outer man until the time of judgment. That is when Jesus will raise the dead. At that time he will raise, and change our bodies. There will be a physical regeneration of the outer man which will be similar to and compatible with the regeneration that took place with the inner man. But be sure not to miss the fact that not everyone will be raised in this manner. Only those who have been spiritually regenerated and sealed by the Spirit of the Lord will experience this physical regeneration.

We can see evidence of this kind of resurrection illustrated in life. For example; a plant and its seed. The seed which represents the death of the plant goes into the ground and eventually brings forth not another seed but a plant that bears fruit, life. Resurrection can also be seen in the transformation of the caterpillar to the butterfly. The caterpillar goes into the cocoon and the first body dies. It then comes out as a butterfly with the beauty and freedom it never had before. But the best example of resurrection is the resurrection of Jesus himself! The body he rose with was changed dramatically from what he went into the grave with.

It is said that, "At the time of the Lord's return he will change our bodies to be like his resurrected body".[7]

Again, I want to point out that understanding these facts, how the law of sin and death and the law of the Spirit of life work, doesn't cause a person to pass from death to life. Simply knowing these facts to be true doesn't cause a regeneration of either the outer or inner man. Merely attesting to the facts, "Ya, that's correct," doesn't change a thing. So the question remains, "what must we do" to receive eternal life?

---

[7] Philippians 3:20,21

Earned Wages

vs.

Free Gifts

Earned Wages vs. Free Gifts

In this chapter I'm going to compare two things, something earned; a wage, with something that is free; a gift. The reason for this comparison is because there is a common misconception among many people that if you do certain things and don't do other things, somehow it qualifies a person to receive eternal life. In other words, the requirements have been met to gain a pass into heaven. The misconception is by doing the dos (going to church, giving money to charities, obeying the ten commandments, helping the elderly cross the street, rescuing a cat from a tree, observance of religious sacraments or liturgy, and things that would be associated with someone referred to as a good person) and not doing the "Thou shalt nots" (adultery, drunkeness, murder, stealing, lying, and things associated with someone viewed as a bad person) that a person is somehow righteous in the sight of God and therefore is awarded eternal life and an entrance into the kingdom of God. Remember the rich young ruler asked Jesus, "What good thing must I do to have eternal life?" He incorrectly believed that eternal life was based on the things he did or didn't do.

This common misconception that eternal life can be earned by doing more good things than bad makes sense in many ways but is a logical impossibility and I'll show you why. When we speak of doing good things and not doing bad things the word "works" is used. Works is by definition a behavioral performance. When we say we will go to heaven because we are basically a good person then we are implying that eternal life is based on our performance. I think many arrive at this incorrect conclusion because most of our experiences in life work that way. We go to work and do what is required and in return we receive wages. These wages are thus earned. The wage is required of the employer to the employee because of a pre arranged agreement. It is a debt of obligation to the employer. The problem with this concept is if eternal life comes by performance then God owes us eternal life.[8] This life is an obligatory debt that is demanded of God because of our performance and is not a gift (grace) but an earned wage (works). Here are some passages that speak to this;

...For it is by grace you have been given eternal life through faith, and this is not from yourselves it is the gift of God, not by works so that no one can boast.

Ephesians 2:8,9

---

[8] Romans 4:1-8

...know that a person is not justified by the works of the law, but by faith in Jesus Christ.... For I do not make void nor insult the grace of God: for if righteousness comes by works, then Jesus died in vain.

Galatians 2:16,21

Notice the last statement, "If righteousness comes by works, then Jesus died in vain." The obvious conclusion (to me) is that if I can attain to eternal life by doing more good things than bad things, then Jesus died in vain. His death was not necessary. He could save others and raise the dead but He couldn't save Himself?

On the other hand (from works), grace is called a gift and a gift is free. You don't do something to receive it and it is not given because of an obligation. Here is an example; If I were to say to you, "I have a new car which I want to give you as a gift" All you would have to do is decide if you want the gift or not. You could say, "Yes, thank you", and take the keys and the title, or you could say something like, "No thanks. I'm happy with the car I have." You could accept or reject the gift. You wouldn't have to earn it, just receive it. It would be free, a free gift.

So if eternal life is indeed a gift from God as Jesus said then it is free and not earned. God is not under an obligation to give someone eternal life just because the someone says He is.

Another form of the earned life concept goes something like this. There is a sort of bench mark for the amount of righteousness required to receive eternal life. Our works get us part of the way there and our faith makes up the difference, or the other way around; the amount of faith that we lack is subsidized by our good works.

The problem with this is, both concepts still arrive at a place where God owes us and that is not how it works. Here is the misconception put into a mathematical equation;

Faith + Works = Eternal life

I have discovered that this is even taught in some churches but is incorrect. The equation would look more accurate written;

Faith (evidenced by works) = Eternal life.

The ridiculousness of the faith plus works concept can be seen in this end game hypothetical. You worked all of your life trying to do more good things than bad but you came up three dollars short on your giving and thus missed out on the blessing of eternal life and the celebration in the kingdom of God. What a shame. Three dollars short. See the picture? This method also leaves the one trying to be good enough with the problem of never knowing if he or she has done enough. They can never be sure if they have eternal life. From our first chapter we know that John wrote, "I write these things so you can <u>KNOW</u> that you <u>HAVE</u> eternal life." Not "guess" or "will have some day", but have eternal life right now and know it!

Now I'd like to use another illustration to provide a way to see the impossibility of eternal life by a means of works or, trying to be "good enough" to make it into the kingdom of God. It would be like trying to be good enough to swim from California to Japan. A person could be an Olympic gold medalist in distance events, even a world record holder, but if they have to swim the San Francisco to Tokyo distance it becomes irrelevant how good they are because, in that hypothetical they could never be good enough.[9] That's the problem with the works approach to eternal life, it's impossible. We can't be good enough.

---

[9] Romans 3:10, 23

Another way to look at this is from the observational conclusion arrived at from our examination of the law of sin and death. The point was made in that chapter but I feel a need to state it again. If we are spiritually dead because of sin which of us can make ourselves spiritually alive again by doing some good thing? In other words, can a dead man bring himself back to life by doing something good? I don't think so. Can you see the impossibility?

Again, just having the understanding of these facts doesn't cause a dead man to come back to life. Merely understanding that eternal life is a gift from God, and not a debt placed upon God doesn't cause us to pass from death to life either.

The remedy to the law of sin and death does not come by intellectual understanding, however understanding the facts is important because it is the place in which we start on the journey to eternal life.

Our original text from John says, "He who has the Son has life." John also said, "...to as many as receive Him He has given the power to become children of God" and heirs according to the promises of Jesus. So how do I receive Him? How do I become a "He who has the Son?" I will address this in more detail in a later chapter but right now I'm hoping you will contemplate these questions.

In the next chapter we will look at who Jesus is, who did he claim to be and who did others think he was? The reason for this is because knowing Jesus is where eternal life comes from. Paul said, "I have many credentials but count them as nothing in the face of knowing Jesus and the power of His resurrection."[10] So how do I get to know Him? Good question right? We will examine this also in a later chapter. One final note; knowing about Jesus and knowing Him are two distinctly different things. I can know the story line (He died for my sins and He rose from the dead) and yet still not know Him. So like Paul, I want to know Him, and I think that starts with.....who did Jesus claim to be?

---

[10] Philippians 3:3-10

Who Do You Say I Am

Who Do You Say I Am?

When Jesus came to the region of Caesarea Philippi, he asked his disciples, "Who do people say the Son of Man is?" They replied, "Some say John the Baptist; others say Elijah; and still others, Jeremiah or one of the prophets." "But what about you?" he asked. "Who do you say I am?" Simon Peter answered, "You are the Messiah, the Son of the living God."
Matthew 16:13-16

If eternal life comes from Jesus then we need to answer the question, "who is Jesus?" Is everyone by definition speaking of the same person? When Jesus asked, "who do people say I am" the response was different from person to person. Some thought He was a prophet. In other places of the gospels people saw Him as merely a good person or a good teacher. Others however saw Him as evil, someone who was born out of fornication, someone who had a demon, "possessed of the devil." With all of these differing conclusions I feel it is important to figure out who Jesus claimed to be and how His disciples interpreted His claim. How did the Pharisees understand His claim?

First-the Pharisees, the religious leaders. One winter while Jesus was at the temple, many of the Pharisees surrounded Him and demanded, "Tell us clearly. Who do you claim to be? Are you the Messiah?" Jesus proceeded to tell them clearly how He was one with God their Father and that He alone is the giver of eternal life,
the promised Messiah. Immediately the priests took up stones to stone· Him to death but Jesus questioned their actions, "Many miracles I have shown you from my Father, for which of these do you stone Me?" Then the priests answered Him, "We are not stoning you over any miracle but for blasphemy, because you being a man claim to be God!"[11] Jesus was claiming to be God and the Pharisees understood that.

Second-Peter. The same Peter who's statement we opened this chapter with wrote many times in his second letter, "Our Lord and Savior Jesus Christ." But in his opening sentence he replaced the word Lord with the word God and proclaimed, "Our God and Savior Jesus Christ."

Third-Thomas. Thomas was not with the disciples when Jesus appeared to them after His resurrection. Thomas said he wouldn't believe Jesus had risen from the dead unless he saw and touched the wounds from His crucifixion. Jesus appeared to Thomas a week later and Thomas declared, Jesus, "My Lord and my God!"[12]

---

[11] John 10:22-33
[12] John 20:27,28

<u>Fourth-Paul</u>. In his letter to Titus Paul speaks of "God our Savior". I believe it is a reference from the many passages in Isaiah that say there is only one God, and this one God is the only Savior.[13] Paul then says in the next verse, "The Lord Jesus Christ our Savior". He then puts the two together and uses the identical language of Peter and says, "We are looking for that blessed hope, and glorious appearing of 'our great God and Savior Jesus Christ.'"

<u>Fifth-John</u>. In the opening remarks of his gospel account John says, "In the beginning was the Word...and the Word was God....and the Word became flesh and dwelt among us."[14] Many times in his gospel account and in The Revelation, John ascribes titles and attributes to Jesus that can only be attributed to God. Such titles as "I am that I am", "Alpha and Omega, the First and the last", Creator of all things (God created all things), Forgiver of sin (only God can forgive sin) and many others. Without exhausting the subject you can see, that not only the ones who believed Jesus was the Messiah and became his disciples understood Him as claiming to be God, but the ones who didn't believe Him and were opposed to Him understood his claim to be God as well. Now with this fact in mind I want to move forward.

---

13 Isaiah 43:10,11/ 45:21
14 John 1:1,14

Jesus asked, "Who do you say I am" because the answer is important. Here's an example which I hope will help us see why. I have a friend who has a landscaper working for him named Jesus. They pronounce his name hey-soose. This Jesus cannot give me eternal life. He can not cause me to pass from death to life. Only the historical, resurrected Jesus of Nazareth, can do this. If by definition I'm relying on some other person named Jesus to give me life and raise me from the dead then I'm out of luck. It's not going to happen. Someone might say, "Isn't it just a matter of semantics? Aren't you just splitting hairs, or being petty?" No, not really. Jesus placed serious importance on getting this right. Even Michael the Archangel, just because I call him Jesus, can't raise the dead or give eternal life.

In the decades following the resurrection of Jesus His disciples addressed on many occasions the necessity of correctly understanding who Jesus is and what their gospel message was. Some groups who claimed to be disciples of the Lord came teaching different things about His resurrection and who Jesus was. They changed the gospel message by claiming there is no resurrection or that it had already happened. Here is how Paul addressed this problem;

I am amazed that you are so quickly deserting Him who called you by the grace of Christ for a different gospel, which is really not the gospel. Evidently some people are throwing you into confusion and are trying to pervert the gospel of Christ. But even if an angel from heaven should preach a gospel other than the one we preached to you, let them be accursed! As we have already said, so now I say again: If anybody is preaching to you a gospel contrary to what you received from us, let them be accursed!

Galatians 1:6-9

On another occasion about a decade later, Paul addressed this issue in a similar fashion.

...I am afraid that, as the serpent deceived Eve by his craftiness, your minds will be led astray from simplicity that is in Christ, by one who preaches another Jesus whom we have not preached, or who brings a different spirit which you have not received of us, or teaches a different gospel which you did not receive from us .....For such men who preach these things are false apostles, deceitful workers, disguising themselves as apostles of Christ. No wonder, for even Satan disguises himself as an angel of light. Therefore it is not surprising if his servants also disguise themselves as servants of righteousness.
II Corinthians 11:3,4,13-15

The importance to the first followers of Jesus about who He claimed to be and what the gospel message was is evident in these scripture citations. This historical documentation makes it clear that the identity of Jesus is critical to our understanding of the gospel, and ultimately the receiving of eternal life. Understanding who He is becomes one of the first steps in getting to know Him.

I touched on "getting to know Him" briefly in the close of the last chapter. I'm bringing it up again because the better I get to know Him the easier it becomes to actually hear from Him, to hear His voice.

There is a very real method of spiritual communication that Jesus uses in His interaction with us. Jesus said, "I am the Good Shepherd and my sheep know my voice. My sheep hear my voice because they know me. They follow me and I give them eternal life."[15] This truth still exists today. Communication is a feature of relationships and is why Jesus communicates with us in the spirit; "They hear my voice". He desires a relationship with us. His goal isn't to have a bunch of robots obeying his commands but to have us hear Him and trust Him. He wants us to allow Him to be the guiding force in our lives. That is what faith is; trusting God. In the next chapter I want to look at the illustrations Jesus used to show the relationship of one person or thing to another, and how these play themselves out in real life. What type of relationship does the Lord want to have with us?

---

[15] John 10:2-4, 14-16, 26-28

Illustrations of the
Relationship

Illustrations of the Relationship

We have now come to what I consider a very important part of the discussion on the subject of eternal life. Here we will review God's desire for an intimate relationship with us. God's will for our lives. I think I can safely say that God wants us to interact with Him and to trust Him. As we travel down life's road together with Him we get to know Him better and develop an understanding of his character. Doing this gives us reasons and evidence for trusting Him. We can trust Him because we know how He sees us; as the affection of his eye. We begin to understand that we were created for his pleasure, He loves us.[16] He wants daily interaction with us not our observance of religious liturgy or rituals.

Here are some biblical examples of relationships and how they illustrate for us those things that make for a personal relationship with the Lord.

Physician-Patient
In Luke 5:30-32 we see Jesus modeling a physician patient relationship. Jesus says the people who see themselves as righteous don't have a need for a doctor. So His purpose is not to come to them as the Great Physician (they don't need healing),

---

[16] Deuteronomy 32:10/ John 13:1/ Revelation 4:11

but to come to those who see themselves honestly and know that they need healing. Spiritual healing. The passing from death to life. This illustration shows that people who are sick go to the doctor and people who aren't (or think they're not) don't. The Great Physician can only heal those who are willing to admit they have a problem and come to Him to be healed. Those who don't know or refuse to admit they are terminal wait until it is too late. With Jesus however it is not too late as long as you are breathing, but why wait? No one knows when their time will be up, right?

Father-Son

These next two illustrations depict a lot of truth. I can identify myself with both of them. Jesus used the illustration of the relationship between fathers and their children many times to paint an emotional picture. In my own life He continually teaches me about my relationship with Him by revealing things to me that exist in my relationship with my son. Many times I have watched my son make mistakes in his life by not listening to the wisdom of his father. I grieve as he brings unnecessary hardships upon himself by not listening. It pains me because I always see him as my son who I love so deeply. In the midst of this, on many occasions, God has spoken to me, "and that is how I feel towards you when you don't listen to Me....only I love you thousands of times more."

The best parable Jesus used in describing the father son relationship is found in Luke's gospel account, 15:11-32. In this story of two sons the emphasis is put on the prodigal. This son decided he knew more than his father and demanded his inheritance so he could go into the world and make his own decisions; become his own man. The parable tells us that the son took his inheritance and squandered it rather quickly on a new found lascivious or as some translations say, riotous life style. The son eventually ran out of money and times got hard. He was lucky to find a job feeding pigs and cleaning their excrement from the pens. This job didn't pay well and soon the son had to resort to eating the husks that were fed to the pigs. One day the son came to his senses and realized that the servants in his father's house had all of their needs met and were never hungry. At this point the son realized he had blown it and should have listen to his father and remained in his father's house. So he decided he would humble himself and go back to his father and confess his stupidity. He went back to his father and said, "Father I have sinned in your sight and am not worthy to be called your son anymore, but just let me be as one of your servants in your household." As the son was finishing the father said, "Don't worry, all is for-given." The father then called his servants to throw a great feast, to put a robe and shoes on the son and to rejoice because, "My son was dead and is alive again, he was lost and now is found!"

In this parable the young man never at any time ceased to be the father's son. The father watched every day for the son to come home. That's what the father wanted, for the son to come home because the father wanted the best things for his son. So also it is with God. He says to us, "Come home to me I have great plans for you." The desire from the son to be right with his father again and return to him was all it took. He didn't have to do penance or perform acts of contrition, only repent, which means turn back to the father.

Groom-Bride

Throughout the bible the followers of Jesus are referred to as the "Bride of Christ". Many times we are described as being married to Him or more accurately, being His fiancee. There is a future event referred to as the marriage supper of the Lamb (Jesus), that will take place just before his return to earth. I think marriage is used as a biblical illustration because it depicts the covenant relationship that exists between Jesus, and his loved ones.

There are a few things to note at the beginning of the marriage relationship and they are; Love is a free choice. God wants us to choose him out of the true desire of our heart. Freely choose to be loved by Him, not because He's bigger and stronger than us but because He loves us and we want to be loved by Him.

Another thing to notice is; Love demands a response. The person being propositioned in a marriage proposal has to respond either yes or no. Maybe is still a no. Even though it's a "not right now" answer, with the possibility of a future yes, it is still a no.

In God's relationship with us He absolutely honors our choice. If we choose to know Him and be loved by Him He honors it. If we choose not to know Him or be close to Him, He honors that. Jesus gives those who choose His love the Holy Spirit as an engagement ring. His Spirit indwells each believer and seals us until the appointed time of the marriage celebration; our resurrection from the dead.[17] Oh, and one more thing; the word divorce does not exist in the vocabulary between Jesus and His bride. He will never divorce us. He will never leave us or forsake us.[18]

<u>Shepherd-Sheep</u> (Psalm 23)
In the gospel of John chapter ten, Jesus refers to Himself as the Good Shepherd, and to us as his sheep. This typology is used by Him because of most people's familiarity with the twenty third Psalm.....It goes like this;

---

[17] Ephesians 1:13,14
[18] Joshua 1:5

The Lord is my shepherd, I lack nothing. He makes me lie down in green pastures; He leads me beside still waters. He restores my soul; He guides me in the paths of righteousness for His name's sake. Yea though I walk through the valley of the shadow of death I fear no evil, for You are with me Lord. Your rod and Your staff, they comfort me. You prepare a table before me in the presence of my enemies. You have anointed my head with oil; My cup overflows. Surely goodness and mercy will follow me all the days of my life, and I will dwell in the house of the Lord forever.

Psalm 23

In this Psalm it is self evident that The Lord like a Good Shepherd, cares for, protects, provides, restores, comforts, guides in all truth and makes it so his sheep will be forever in his kingdom. So with that in mind as I examine John chapter ten I see the parallels with the words of Jesus found there and with the twenty third Psalm. Jesus claims to be the Good Shepherd of Psalm twenty three and adds to it that He is willing to sacrifice his life for his sheep, that He will die for them.[19] Just as I stated at the end of the last chapter Jesus said his sheep know his voice, they trust Him and they follow Him. This reaction to the good shepherd is part of the process of getting to know Him in this capacity. One other point that is evident from John ten is, not only do we follow Him because we know his voice but He knows us by our name and calls us accordingly.

---

[19]John 10:11,15

In another parable about sheep and a good shepherd Jesus gives the example of a shepherd that has a hundred sheep but looses one of them. He leaves the ninety nine other sheep secure then goes to pursue the one that got lost.[20] Similar to the prodigal son we examined in a previous illustration, there is great rejoicing when the lost comes back home. When the one is found. In this illustration however we see that the lost is actually pursued by the Good Shepherd. The relationship depicted by these examples of sheep and a good shepherd is obvious to me and needs little explanation other than; it's his desire to do these things for his sheep. Jesus wants to, and is able to do these things. He is more than able to give eternal life and resurrection from the dead.

Friend-Friend
Friendship is another relationship that is used as an example of how Jesus wants to interact with us. A friend is much different than a disciplinarian or a drill sergeant. A friend is personal. A friend has your back and will be there when you need help. A friend is free of charge and doesn't expect payment. A friend thinks about you continually. Jesus said, "No greater thing can a man do than lay down his life for a friend. And I call you friends and not servants, for you are my friends."[21] He talks about laying down his life in a sacrificial way for his followers. This is the greatest thing He can do according to Him.

---

[20]Luke 15:3-7
[21]John 15:13-15

In the Old Testament there is a passage I am intrigued with. It is Exodus 33:11. In this story Moses would go to the mountain top and hear from God. He would then go and tell the Israelites what God had said. In this Exodus passage it says that, "God spoke to Moses face to face as a friend speaks to his friend." I am amazed at the reference, face to face. I think that's how the Lord wants to speak to us, face to face as a friend speaks to a friend. Today this face to face happens in a spiritual way but I think it will be realized in a literal physical way in the future. Can you imagine speaking with Jesus face to face?

<u>Judge-Defendant</u> (Legal)
This is a very different type of relationship from the others. I thought it would be good to examine because of the large content of laws contained in the Bible, and because there is much spoken of in the Bible in legal language. In getting to the point of this trial type relationship it would be best to view Jesus as the prosecuting attorney. He tells the judge (the Father) if the case against the defendant (us) is going to be tried or dismissed. A person can only have the charges against them forgiven by going through the prosecuting attorney. Jesus said, "*NO ONE* comes to the Father *EXCEPT* through me."[22]

---

[22]John 14:6

The relationship here can be either one of peace and friendship or adversarial with animosity. The important part is; God lets us choose where we stand and then honors our choice. That's what love does. If I choose an adversarial relationship with Him then I perceive judgment in his words. If I choose an allied relationship with Him I perceive forgiveness, grace, and mercy.

Teacher-Student

Jesus spoke to his disciples just before his death and told them about the Holy Spirit that He would soon give them.[23] He told them the Holy Spirit would speak to them and they would hear Him. Jesus claimed the Holy Spirit would guide them and teach them, and would instruct them in all truth. He said the Holy Spirit would even show them mysteries, things to come in the future. It is the Holy Spirit that convicts us of sin, and gives us a conscious. He tells us when we deviate from God's will. He teaches us to recognize when this happens. We are always learning from Him and sometimes He gives us a surprise test. The results of these tests reveal to us the growth in our spiritual relationship with Jesus, and how much we do or don't trust Him.

Many times the Bible refers to the Lord as speaking to us through his Spirit. When we experience this we should always remember that He will never contradict what is written in scripture when He speaks. If a contradiction with

---

[23] John 16:13

scripture arises then we can be sure that we are not hearing Him accurately.

So while we wait to see Him face to face we are constantly learning and He is continually teaching. He speaks to us through his word, the New Testament, but we speak to each other through prayer. Not prayer that has to have some liturgical preamble, or some magic words at the end, but a real conversation. Not just reflecting on my requests or my needs, but grateful for our relationship and for who He is and how He has called me out of darkness into his light. Not just hearing myself speak, but hearing Him speak too.

There are other biblical illustra-tions of relationships but I thought these would be enough to work with. I feel that these are sufficient to show an interaction between God and man. Just as Jesus was always praying and in commun-ication with the one He called our Father, we should use the example from his life and be in constant communication with Him.

Again as I conclude this chapter I want to reiterate, simply knowing these facts and information doesn't cause us to pass from death to life. So someone might say at this point, "Enough already! Tell me plainly, what does cause a person to pass from death to life? How is it done? What must I do?" In the next chapter I will finally give the answer.

I have spent a lot of time presenting information and then telling my readers that the information doesn't accomplish the thing we are seeking. But now I will tell you in a clear way what we must do to receive eternal life and pass today, from death to life.

What Should I Do

What Should I do?

<u>Repent</u>

In the previous chapters I have spent a lot of time presenting information about eternal life, the false notion that we can somehow earn it and the spiritual laws associated with it that affect us. By this time we should know that we don't do anything to earn eternal life, but hopefully we are also aware that we have to do more than just agree with the facts. Using a baseball analogy; we don't throw our glove on the field and say we win, but we have to put that glove on and go onto the field and play the game. In other words, there is an action associated with faith. If I truly believe then there should be a response to that belief. For example: if I believe the bridge is sound I will use it to cross the river. So what we have come to now I would call our reaction. How will I react to what I have just read in the previous chapters of this book?

The action word that was used in the sermons of the Apostles, and should still be used today is repentance. In the historical document called "The Acts of the Apostles", Peter and Paul continually told their listeners to repent. As I bring attention to this word I want to first give it definition because of the misconceptions I associated with it most of my life. When I heard "repent", I always had a view of a mean and angry God who was threatening me with harm and wanted to scare me to death. In my world the word repent carried with it a view of a God who wanted to hurt me or rip me off, not of someone who loves me. So how does my vine's dictionary define the word repent, or repentance?

Repent, Repentance

Verb, metanoeo

lit., "to perceive afterwards" (meta, "after," implying "change," noeo, "to perceive;" nous, "the mind, the seat of moral reflection"), in contrast to pronoeo, "to perceive beforehand," hence signifies "to change one's mind or purpose," always, in the NT, involving a change for the better, an amendment, and always, except in Luke 17:3,4, of "repentance" from sin. The word is found in the Synoptic Gospels, in Luke nine times, in Acts five times, in the Apocalypse twelve times. In the New Testament the subject chiefly has reference to "repentance" from sin, and this change of mind involves both a turning from sin and a turning to God. The parable of the Prodigal Son is an outstanding illustration of this.

So as I see it the definition of repent is a literal changing of my mind, turning from sin and turning to God. If as in chapter two sin is the obliquity or deviation from God's plan or purpose then repentance is the returning to God's plan or purpose. Sin is in a sense missing the mark and turning <u>FROM GOD</u>, and repentance is a turning <u>TO GOD</u>. In my experience I have seen this turning to God evidenced in a crying out to Him. This desire to be right with God manifests even if the avenue in which to travel isn't evident to the penitent person or, the strength to repent is elusive and hard to find. Please note that repentance will always accompany true faith, they are insepar-able. As in the bridge analogy, if I truly believe I will act upon what I believe.

Confession of Faith

This brings me to my next point. When this repentance takes place it should be accompanied by some form of a confession of that faith. The reason why I believe a confession of faith should accompany repentance and true faith, is found in a very clearly stated passage of Romans;

......But what does it say? "The word is near you; it is _in your mouth_ and _in your heart_," that is, the message concerning faith that we proclaim: If you declare _with your mouth_, "Jesus is Lord," and believe _in your heart_ that God raised him from the dead, you will be saved. For it is _with your heart_ that you believe and are justified, and it is _with your mouth_ that you profess your faith and are saved. As Scripture says, "Anyone who believes in him will never be put to shame." For there is no difference between Jew and Gentile, the same Lord is Lord of all and richly blesses all who _call on him_, for, "_Everyone who calls on the name of the Lord will be saved._"

Romans 10:8-13

From these verses we can see that what we believe in the heart will be manifested in a verbal confession of the mouth. Many times Jesus claimed things like, "Out of the abundance of the heart the mouth speaks."[24] In other words the mouth will declare the things that are in the heart. That's why when the heart is desperate to be right with God the mouth can't help but cry out.

---

24 Luke 6:45

Jesus said, "If you will confess me before men I will confess you before the Father who is in heaven, but if you deny me before men I will deny you before the Father who is in heaven." He also said, "For every word a man speaks he shall give an account. For by your words you shall be justified and by your words you shall be condemned."[25] The power of life and death reside in the tongue. It is like the rudder of a ship that steers the soul.

When I have a deep desire in my heart, or I am deeply in love with someone, there is a sense in my heart that I want to tell other people. I want to confess, "I love this woman" or "I love this man." In the same kind of way my heart should get to a point where I can't contain it and I have to declare, "Jesus! I want Jesus. I believe He is alive and I want Him in my life." At this point He comes and lives in me. Remember from chapter three how the Spirit of the Lord affects the inner man? We become one spirit with the Lord. Remember Jesus saying, "Ask and you shall receive, seek and you shall find....If earthly fathers know how to give good gifts, how much more will our heavenly Father give the Holy Spirit to those who ask?" When this happens The Spirit of the Lord dwells in us and we become one spirit with Him. We are sealed with the Holy Spirit until the day of our resurrection. At this point we "HAVE" the Son. We have received him[26].

---

[25] Matthew 10:32,33 and Matthew 12: 36,37

[26] John 1:12

Now, remember the first scripture we reviewed in the first chapter on page eighteen, ..."he who has the Son has life"? At the point when you become one spirit with the Lord you have the Son, YOU HAVE THE SON! You have (present tense) eternal (forever) life. You have passed (past tense) from death to life! So now you know! Now you can know for certain if you have the Son and you have eternal life! "I write these things to you who believe so YOU CAN KNOW that you have eternal life."

Spiritual Warfare

Spiritual Warfare

Spiritual warfare is a subject that I need to address at this point in our discussion because of how it directly affects our decision making process when God is calling us to receive eternal life. It is called warfare because it is a war designed to keep us from the love of God and to destroy our soul. Spiritual warfare is something that is constantly going on even though it is hard to see with our natural eyes. This warfare is like the wind. We can't see wind and we don't know where it comes from or where it goes, but if it moves fast enough we are aware of its effects. This is also true with spiritual warfare. I can't even tell you what dimensions it crosses into, but I know by scripture and by my experiences that it influences us in this time and space in which we live and is very real. Just because we haven't been aware of it or sensed it doesn't mean it does not exist. So maybe I should define what I mean by spiritual warfare.

I think this term can best be described as the conflict that is ongoing in the unseen realm between the person of hatred and death (Satan) and the person of love and life (Jesus). Each side uses what we call angels as their executors. The angels battle one another in order to carry out the will of the person of their allegiance. Angels are spirits and this warfare takes place in the spiritual realm. It is actuated in the minds and hearts of men. The devil (who I will refer to as the adversary) has an agenda and a strategy. His agenda includes;

1) The lie that he, the adversary and his warfare don't exist
2) Cause us to doubt the things that God has said
3) Cause us to question God's motives
4) Attempt to destroy God's creation
5) Cause man to sin and die
6) To ultimately be exalted and worshiped as greater than God

OK, lets examine number five on the list above. This ongoing warfare creates a paradox in the minds and hearts of most people that is experienced like this. Sometimes you are curious and want to know God, and be closer to Him, and yet at times you want to distance yourself from Him, don't want to hear it. What is that? What's going on when this is happening? Have you ever experienced these two things? There are two spiritual opponents, if you will, pulling on the strings of our hearts. One is pulling us to enter into the love of God, and to experience the peace and joy that it brings and ultimately receive eternal life, while the other is pulling us to fulfill a natural desire. The adversary uses the lust of the flesh and the pride of man to cause us to try and find fulfillment in the deceitfulness of riches and temporary pleasures of the world. We get fooled by the mirage that is orchestrated by him, designed to direct us away from the love of God. Its purpose is to get us to chase after something or some situation that has the illusion of holding the answer to long term happiness, peace, and contentment. This is designed to lead us away from what truly brings these things which are only found in a relationship with Jesus. Since eternal life can only come from Jesus, the adversary wants to keep us from the Lord so that he can kill us, destroy our soul, and keep us so we never pass from death to life. He can't pull a gun out and shoot us, he has to get us to make the wrong choice.

The reaction of Adam and Eve after they disobeyed God and partook of the tree is a common reaction of men. It is a good example of how the adversary gets us to create distance with God. When we do something contrary to what we know God's will is, we tend to hide from Him like Adam and Eve did. But just as disobedience causes us to hide or withdraw from God, serious tribulation forces us to search for Him. I've even heard a professing atheist in a time of great distress say something like, "Oh God why is this happening", or "Oh God no! Don't let this happen to me." Even the person who gives very little thought to God, will wonder about God and what happens when you die, when a loved one dies, or when they or someone close to them is diagnosed with a terminal illness. Just as in the story of the prodigal son, when life's situations get bad enough we tend to cry out to God. Sometimes however, realizing the depth of God's love accomplishes the same thing; repentance, turning to Him.

If it were as easy as receiving a gift why wouldn't everyone sign up to receive the gift of eternal life? Spiritual warfare keeps them from it that's why. It is as easy as receiving a gift but the enemy of our souls keeps us from it by stirring up human pride. We experience an inability to bow the knee or raise the hand to God because of our stupid pride. Pride makes us unable to say, "Yes Lord, please forgive me." As ignorant as it sounds, pride makes us resistant to the gift of eternal life. And as I think about it, this isn't a matter of a lack of intelligence but an issue of our ego.

Books and volumes of books have been written on the subject of spiritual warfare. The specific aspect of this subject I have chosen to write about was done with the desire to illustrate how spiritual warfare is designed to keep us from a relationship with God. I wanted to expose how it works to cause us to believe lies about God's motives and promises. I thought it might be good however to give a short list of scriptures for anyone who might want more information on this subject. So here are some scriptures that speak about spiritual warfare and the combatants.

......Finally, my brethren, be strong in the Lord and in the power of His might. Put on the whole armor of God, that you may be able to stand against the wiles of the devil. For we do not wrestle against flesh and blood, but against principalities, against powers, against the rulers of the darkness of this age, against spiritual hosts of wickedness in the heavenly places.

Ephesians 6:10-12

.....For though we walk in the flesh, we do not war according to the flesh. For the weapons of our warfare are not carnal but mighty in God for pulling down strongholds, casting down arguments and every high thing that exalts itself against the knowledge of God, bringing every thought into captivity.....

II Corinthians 10:3-5

.....I say then: Walk in the Spirit, and you shall not fulfill the lust of the flesh. For the flesh lusts against the Spirit, and the Spirit against the flesh; and these are contrary to one another, so that you do not do the things that you wish....

Galatians 5:16-23

These scriptures speak about the adversary and his motives

I Peter 5:8...The devil is like a lion searching for prey

John 8:42-44...He is a murderer and the father of lies

John 10:6-10...He is a thief come to steal life

These speak about the war and interaction of angels and demons

Hebrews 1:13,14...Angels minister to believers

Revelation 12:7-9...War between Michael the archangel and Satan

Revelation 20:1-3...Again Satan and demons bound by angels

Daniel 10:1-14...Demon prevents angel from coming to Daniel

Even if we don't count all of the exorcisms and demon possessions in the Bible these references make it clear there is definitely something going on in the spiritual realm. I am sharing this in an effort to expose the deception of the adversary. I hope the reader will see that there is something at work trying to keep them from Jesus. There is an attempt to use a person's egotistical pride to keep them from receiving the free gift of eternal life. In the last chapter I hope I was able to make it clear how you can receive eternal life. In the next chapter I am going to share my own transformation experience. I am hoping there might be something in it that makes the concept of passing from death to life a reality for you like it is for me.

A Love Story

A Love Story!

For God so loved the world that He gave His only begotten Son, that whoever believes in Him should not perish but have everlasting life. For God did not send His Son into the world to condemn the world, but that the world through Him might pass from death to life.

John 3:16

The main point of the New Testament is this, "God loves us." I find this truth present on all of its pages. I feel He wants me to be sure of this fact, to be sure that his motive in all that He does is one of love. As I read the words of Jesus and the rest of the New Testament I realize I am reading a love story. But not just any love story, it's the greatest love story ever! Scripture says that even while we were opposed to Jesus, maybe even shaking our fist at Him, or angry with Him, even in our indifference, before we were born, Jesus demonstrated His love for us by dying and making a provision for us to be able to pass from death to life.[27] When we talk about love what are we saying?

The New Testament defines it as choices, not just an emotional feeling.

Love is;

---

[27] Romans 5:8

Patient
Kind
Not envious
Not boastful
Humble
Polite
Not selfish
Not easily angered
Forgiving
Honest
Protecting
Trusting
Hopeful
Enduring[28]

Most of this list is behavior we have to make a conscious effort to do. In many cases these choices don't come naturally. On the other hand it is written that God is love. This is what He is by nature so these come naturally to Him, these are his attributes. Look at the list again. Is this how you see God? Patient, kind, forgiving, and compassionate, or angry and vindictive? Which observation do you think is correct? Ya, me too. Scripture says that God not only loves but is love, and that perfect love casts out fear because fear has torment.[29] So God is not trying to get us to respond to Him by threatening us or trying to scare us but by loving us. As I said before, "Love demands a response." We have to make a choice and respond to God's love by saying either yes or no.

---

[28] I Corinthians 13:4-7
[29] I John 4:16-18

I want to share with you my choice, my personal experience in responding to the love of God. The date when I finally said "I do" to the propositioning of God was May 1, 1988. It was a day like no other and I will never forget the experience. But before I tell you about this day I need to share with you what was going on in my life up to that point so you can understand just how emotional and powerful this day was. My life was such that I had everything. At least everything the world says is important. I was 32 years old, and in great physical health. I owned multiple pieces of real estate that were appreciating at a furious pace. I owned new cars and trucks. I was married and had a wonderful son. I had nice clothes, new furniture and terrific friends. I played in a band and I had access to the best marijuana around. I had all of this and more yet something wasn't right. There was something missing but I wasn't sure what, or why I hadn't reached nirvana if you will, considering my situation. One day it got to me and I cried out, "God if you're real and you can hear me show yourself, answer me! If you really exist and you can hear me, I dare you to show your face. I'll meet you at that church over by the softball field tomorrow at high noon. Be there if you're not a coward!" Can you imagine this? Me calling out God like I'm Jesse James? Can you feel my frustration? I was frustrated with not being able to understand the meaning and purpose of my life. I'm glad God has a sense of humor. Believe it or not I think He got a good laugh out of my imbecilic behavior.

So Sunday May 1 came and I went to church (a place I never went). After the music the preacher got up and started teaching from the Bible. I can't remember what he said or what passages he was teaching from but I was sure of one thing, God was speaking to me through this man as he spoke the words from scripture. It was like the words were alive and cutting right to my heart.[30] I was thinking to myself, "There's no way this guy could know all of these things about me, all of my feelings and circumstances, this has to be God." I remembered back to the different times in my life when something like this had happened before and then it dawned on me, it was God speaking to me back then too. I was shaking like an earthquake while this was going on. I was crying through much of it, but not because I was sad. This was embarrassing for me being the pseudo tuff guy I thought I was. I was messing up my reputation. But what I realized was I was experiencing God embracing me with his love. I was actually feeling the love and presence of God. It was like Jesus himself was hugging me. It was high noon! He showed up! I feel extremely limited in trying to explain this to you in words.
The emotional experience was beyond description.

---

[30] Hebrews 4:12, Romans 10:17

At the end of the service the preacher asked if anyone wanted to respond to his message and give their life to Jesus. I wasn't sure what that meant but I knew that the Spirit of God was compelling me to do that, to get up and go forward. I went to the front of the church and prayed with the preacher and some of the elders from their church. I don't remember what words we prayed but I know at that moment I was changed, transformed, I passed right then from death to life. The Spirit of the Lord performed spiritual heart surgery on me and I was different!

The day after this amazing transformation I got up and car pooled to work with my three other friends like I had always done. I bring this up because I want you to be aware of the immediate difference in my being. As we were driving to work everyone was talking about what they had done that weekend. I was being quiet because I wasn't sure what to say or how it would be received. One of my buddies asked me, "So Gino, anything exciting happen to you on the weekend?" Without thinking I just reacted with a sort of confidence and excitement. "You guys are never going to believe this but I went to church (I was the least likely person to ever do that) and God changed me." I tried to explain to them how I didn't feel like getting high anymore. I didn't have to, not that I wasn't allowed to, but I didn't need to. I told them, "It's like getting paroled and I don't have to go back to doing time in a prison. Jesus changed my life. He lives in me now."

As I was saying these things and trying to explain this amazing experience, I was sort of outside my body listening to myself speak thinking, "What the....Is this me? Where are these words coming from?" It was the same thing that was going on when I heard the preacher on Sunday; God was speaking through me to them! It goes without saying these guys were blown away. They weren't sure how to react. One guy wanted to give me a hard time but it was like he was choking on his words and couldn't confront the wisdom and power of God that was coming out of my mouth. As the days went on the guys razzed me and railed against the God concept but they couldn't argue against the transformation that had taken place in my life. They knew the Gino that was an angry addict, and the new Gino who was much nicer and happier. They knew the Gino that would rage against the Gospel and the Gino that now declared with boldness the Gospel. The old Gino had become a follower of Jesus, yes, a Jesus freak!

After reading this someone might say, "I've tried this before and it didn't work for me." I know that this is a common experience. Many times people don't experience any extreme emotions when they pray a prayer of faith and they think it didn't work. Sometimes people think there is something wrong with them, maybe something unforgivable.

But sometimes transformation doesn't take place because they are coming to God with the wrong motives in their heart, they only want to see what they can get. Maybe they just want a genie in a bottle but really have no desire to know Jesus or have an intimate relationship with Him. For these reasons and others, people will turn away with the sense that it didn't work for them.[31] Remember not everyone's experience is the same. Every person will experience different levels of emotion. A high level of emotion doesn't necessarily reveal spiritual regeneration, and visa versa. If for some reason a person feels "it didn't work", try again. Anything worth having is worth pursuing.

Just as I'm waking in the morning the Spirit of God sometimes gives me inspiration for the things I write. The Spirit of the Lord gave me this story as an illustration of how He feels towards his creation. God created all of us and loves all of us. He wants to bestow the best gifts upon us just as a lord will lavish a princess with exorbitant gifts. Not as much now in the temporary world but soon in the eternal future. This story tells of three different people. The lord represents Jesus, the woman represents us, and the other man represents all of the distractions in the world.

---

[31] Matthew 13:20-22

The young woman was found by the lord cast into a field and left for dead, her body bloody and unwashed. The lord covered her nakedness, took her and cleaned her. He anoints her with the most exotic and intoxicating fragrances. He put diamonds on her neck, ears and hands.[32] Her neck sparkles as her now beautifully restored, thick flowing black hair frames her soft and tender neck and shoulders. Shyness and modesty clothed her beauty. Her style and manner is one of peace and humility accompanied by strength and confidence. As she is pampered in the lord's palace she becomes exceedingly beautiful to the sight. She finds it difficult to receive gifts from the lord because she feels to do so would carry with it an implied obligation of commitment to a relationship with him. She loves the lord and is grateful for all of the wonderful things he has done and continues to do for her but is afraid of the commitment. One day she meets another man and is moved by him. She leaves the lord because she thinks that this other man can give her what she is looking for, unfortunately only to find out later that what she truly wants and needs can only be found in the arms of her first love. She eventually realizes that no one loves her like her lord does. But, when she finally did recognize that the security she desired could only be found in a commitment with her lord, it was too late. She wasn't able to find her way back to him. The lord was crushed with heaviness because the stunningly beautiful one he had created rejected

---

[32] Ezekiel chapter 16

him. Some time after this she became seriously ill. Her new relationship failed. The one who showed her the illusion of love left her for another, shortly after which she died.

What I'm hoping you connect with in this parable is how the lord felt towards the beautiful woman he created. The beautiful one he created and loved is a representation of us. God created you, one person, and he views something stunningly beautiful in his creation. Beauty is in the eye of the beholder and God beholds his creation, you, like no one else. You were created for his pleasure.[33] But have you ever been on God's side of this experience? Have you ever been passionately, romantically, desperately, out of your mind in love with someone? All you can think about is them? You constantly talk about them? All you see is their beauty? Did you ever experience something like this only to have the one you were infatuated with reject you and leave? Or maybe even had them cheat on your love and give that love that you desperately wanted from them to someone else?

---

[33] Revelation 4:11

If you ever had the misfortune of experiencing something like what I just described then I think you can appreciate how Jesus feels when we reject Him. He loves us beyond what we can imagine and wants us to love Him. When we don't make a commitment with Him (for what ever reason) we break his heart. I imagine it is an absolutely crushing experience for Him. Take your rejection experience and multiply it times trillions because, "God so loved.....THE WORLD!" Whether a mate or a child, rejection by someone we love, is for most people an experience that will make them feel sick to their stomach. It can be excruciatingly painful! It can make us despair even of life. So the question is, "How do you think God feels when we reject Him?"

If I were to end my little parable where I did it would be a heartbreaking story. So lets not do that. Here's another ending for the story of the lord and the beautiful woman. This hopefully illustrates why I desperately want to share the message of eternal life with you. The beautiful woman rejected the lord and yes found out she had a terminal illness. But in the midst of her grief and heartache before she died, the beautiful one turns to God and receives eternal life. She committed her life and future to Jesus Christ. At the moment she surrendered her life and love to Him she was transformed and passed from death to life. She became a partaker in the resurrection and entered into the kingdom of God.

One day the beautiful woman was walking in the kingdom of God and could see a person approaching her. Even from a distance she sensed there was something familiar about this person. As he called her name while approaching she realized it was her lord, the love of her life! She wasn't able to have an earthly marriage with him but now she realized what the love of her life was trying to tell her, "That it was more important to him to be able to spend eternity with her in the kingdom of God than a temporary time with her on earth." As she fainted into his arms because of being over-whelmed with joy she remembered her love's words and how he had tried to tell her about the love of God and the way of eternal life so many times. She remem-bered his words and all of the times he tried to explain to her the importance of understanding the message. She realized that it was, in part, because of his persistence that she made a commitment and was able to be in the kingdom of God rejoicing. The man she was unable to enjoy in the temporary life she was able to enjoy in eternal life! The decision she made to commit her life to Jesus turned out to be the best decision she ever made!

This story is a story about the heart. I bring this up because it appears to me that the issue of receiving eternal life is a heart issue. It comes down to; God wants to win over our hearts, but will the pride in our hearts allow him to do that? The Lord said;

My son, pay attention to what I say;
turn your ear to my words.
Do not let them out of your sight,
keep them in the midst of your heart;
for they are life to those who find them
and health to one's whole being.
Above all else, guard your heart,
for out of it flow the issues of life.

Proverbs 4:20-23

Man can't make any judgment about the condition of the heart only God can.[34] The Bible speaks of the heart close to 500 times and implies things about heart issues many more times. It is said that the heart is where sin proceeds from, murders, adulteries, thefts, lies etc. It is where evil thoughts start. It is where hardness and unbelief come from. On the other hand it is said that your heart will be where you store your treasure, the things most important to you. Out of the goodness of the heart the mouth speaks. In other words the mouth reveals what is in the heart.[35]

---

[34] Jeremiah 17:9
[35] Luke 6:45

Besides evil things the heart also produces good things. Love decisions come from the heart and so does the faith that transforms our lives (believe in your **HEART** that Jesus rose from the dead and you will be saved)[36].

It seems the condition of the heart can be quite different from time to time and from person to person, that's why only God can know the heart of man. The evil in our hearts is desperate to not be exposed either. It will try all evasive maneuvers to keep from being found out. God wants to win over our hearts but that would expose our pride. The pride in us that says, "I can do it myself, or I'm a good enough person and a loving God will accept me as I am, or even, I don't need a God."

Unfortunately for that pride there is a hidden desire in our hearts to find and experience unconditional love! Unconditional love is what our hearts are searching for whether we know it or not and this love can only be found with Jesus. This creates that battle or warfare in the heart and our heart is what the Lord wants. Jesus said that the greatest commandment is to love God with all our heart, and when we search for Him with all of our heart He will be found.[37] At that point we confess with our mouth what is in our heart and we pass from death to life. We choose the life that Jesus gives.

---

[36] Romans 10:9
[37] Luke 10:27/ Jeremiah 29:13

If we don't choose life God will honor our choice. One day that person will be giving an account of his life before God and the Lord will open the envelope with that person's name on it.
There will be a slip inside which will be in that person's handwriting and will read something like;
"I don't want anything to do with Jesus". God will honor that choice and send them away. As that person is leaving they will realize that the unconditional love they had searched for their entire life was there with Jesus and they were going to miss out on experiencing that love because of their egotistical pride and hardness of heart (This is only an allegorical illustration).

Ultimately, it all comes down to how I relate to Jesus. Am I trying to relate to Him by religious liturgy or by trust? Does He want someone to know when to stand or kneel in church or someone to know Him? Does He want me to pray memorized words or pray by talking to Him? Am I approaching Him based on the good things that I do or the things He has already done (die in my place so I don't have to, rose from the dead so there's a way I can too)? Am I going to trust Jesus, the one born of a virgin, who is God manifest in the flesh, who rose from the dead and is alive today or am I going to trust myself? Are the things that Jesus said about eternal life and resurrection from the dead true or am I going to trust something else? Which one? "There is a way that might seem right to men but the end of that way is death."[38]

There are many religions in the world that teach many things, but the true wisdom they teach becomes irrelevant if they misrepresent who Jesus is and what He claimed his purpose was for dying and rising from the dead. Eternal life is not about religion. It's not about if your family raised you in a Christian home. It doesn't come from the observance of religious sacraments or traditions. It is something that comes from a heart that trusts God and that wants to know Him. It comes from being real with Him. When we pass from death to life the Lord Jesus lives in us by his spirit. We become one spirit with the Lord. When this happens we "have the Son".

---

[38] Proverbs 14:12

......The testimony of God is this; He has given us eternal life and this life is in his son. <u>He who has the son has life</u>, and he who does not have the son does not have life. <u>I write these things</u> to you who believe **<u>SO YOU CAN KNOW that you have eternal life</u>**.....

I John 5:11-13

I hope I have made this a clear presentation, and that it is now easier than when you started reading, to know if you have eternal life. My motive for writing this is the same as that of John, "So you can know." If for some reason that's not the case then maybe meditate on what you have read. Pray to God and ask Him for clarity. I would also suggest re-reading the chapter titled "What Should I do". My heart's desire for you is that now you are able to answer this question with certainty, "Do you know if you have eternal life?"

Printed in Great Britain
by Amazon

19481399R00061